PENGUIN BOOKS

*Poems and Readings for Funerals*

Julia Watson was born in Wales, and read English and Drama at Exeter University.

Her many television appearances include several series of *Casualty* for the BBC playing Dr Baz – she recently paid a final visit to Holby! – and Thames TV's long-running comedy series *Never the Twain* with Donald Sinden and Windsor Davies. She has worked extensively in theatre, and has appeared in *Danton's Death, Major Barbara, She Stoops to Conquer* and *Wild Honey* for the National Theatre.

In 2003 she received a Grammy nomination (Best Performance) for *The Woman and the Hare* with the Nashe Ensemble.

Julia Watson is married to the poet David Harsent. They live with their daughter in Barnes, south-west London.

S
p

R
E
T
I

# Poems and Readings for Funerals

EDITED BY JULIA WATSON

PENGUIN BOOKS

PENGUIN BOOKS

Published by the Penguin Group
Penguin Books Ltd, 80 Strand, London WC2R ORL, England
Penguin Group (USA), Inc., 375 Hudson Street, New York, New York 10014, USA
Penguin Books Australia Ltd, 250 Camberwell Road, Camberwell, Victoria 3124, Australia
Penguin Books Canada Ltd, 10 Alcorn Avenue, Toronto, Ontario, Canada M4V 3B2
Penguin Books India (P) Ltd, 11 Community Centre, Panchsheel Park, New Delhi – 110 017, India
Penguin Books (NZ) Ltd, Cnr Rosedale and Airborne Roads, Albany, Auckland, New Zealand
Penguin Books (South Africa) (Pty) Ltd, 24 Sturdee Avenue, Rosebank 2196, South Africa

Penguin Books Ltd, Registered Offices: 80 Strand, London WC2R ORL, England

www.penguin.com

Published in Penguin Books 2004
3

This collection copyright © Julia Watson, 2004
The acknowledgements on pp. 107–9 constitute an extension of this copyright page
All rights reserved

The moral right of the editor has been asserted

Set in 11/13 pt PostScript Monotype Garamond
Typeset by Rowland Phototypesetting Ltd, Bury St Edmunds, Suffolk
Printed in England by Clays Ltd, St Ives plc

# Contents

*A tiny lamp has gone out in my tent . . .*

*He was my North, my South, my East and West . . .*

## *Worn features of ancestral mould . . .*

## *To every thing there is a season . . .*

# Foreword

From time to time my husband David Harsent and I are asked for suggestions for readings. As poet and actress respectively, we are thought to know about these things – in reality we have to do the research too. Each occasion has its own specific requirements. Thus the idea for this collection came about.

These poems and readings have been chosen to be read aloud at a service celebrating someone's life, although the very short pieces are also suggestions for inclusion on a printed order of service.

Funerals, unlike weddings, are rarely planned. Even with the knowledge that death may come soon, no one wants to give up hope of that life and organize the sending-off. My father, knowing he was dying, planned his funeral – the readings, music, everything. It gave us, his family, some comfort in those incredibly difficult days following his death to know that we were giving him the exit he wanted.

Sometimes friends who are not used to reading in public come for advice. It is important to be very familiar with the piece. Practise it aloud in private, checking the rhythm if it is a poem, remembering to acknowledge the line breaks and being clear about what it all means. It is often not possible to have a practice in the place where the service is being held, and only in the larger spaces will microphones be offered. The way to ensure that one is speaking loudly enough is to do the reading to the people at the back. This makes one naturally raise the voice. I have attended several services where the readings have been inaudible. A lot of effort has gone into the selection – it is therefore important that the piece is heard. But at the end of the day it is not about the performance; it is all about the celebration of someone's life.

*Julia Watson*

*Remember me when I am gone away . . .*

Seasons turn and rivers flow
Mourn me hard and let me go.

'Last Wish',
Asa James (1972– )

## 'Remember me when I am gone away'

Remember me when I am gone away,
   Gone far away into the silent land;
   When you can no more hold me by the hand,
Nor I half turn to go yet turning stay.
Remember me when no more day by day
   You tell me of our future that you planned:
   Only remember me, you understand
It will be late to counsel then or pray.
Yet if you should forget me for a while
   And afterwards remember, do not grieve:
   For if the darkness and corruption leave
   A vestige of the thoughts that once I had,
Better by far you should forget and smile
   Than that you should remember and be sad.

*Christina Rossetti* (1830–94)

## Heaven-Haven

I have desired to go
 Where springs not fail,
To fields where flies no sharp and sided hail
 And a few lilies blow.

And I have asked to be
 Where no storms come,
Where the green swell is in the havens dumb,
 And out of the swing of the sea.

*Gerard Manley Hopkins* (1844–89)

## Life Goes On

If I should go before the rest of you,
Break not a flower nor inscribe a stone
Nor when I'm gone speak in a Sunday voice
But be the usual selves that I have known.
Weep if you must,
Parting is hell,
But life goes on,
So sing as well.

*Joyce Grenfell* (1910–79)

# Living Each Day

Now I am gone, now I am lost to you
Find me again just as you used to do:

In the house – when you go from room to room you'll find
The bits and pieces that I've left behind.

In the street – of course . . . I've stopped to window-shop;
You carry on, my love, I'll catch you up.

At night – as darkness slowly fills the sky:
I'm late; don't fret; I'll be there by and by.

At morning – when the sky is still blue-black,
I had to go out early: I'll be back.

In sunshine – as you peer into the glare –
A shape that seems to be both light and air.

In rain – as you look out and people pass –
One leaves a reflection printed on the glass.

In the garden – when you doze away the hours
I pass with a smile on my face, and my arms full of flowers.

*Lisa Kitson* (1961– )

## 'Death is nothing at all'

Death is nothing at all. I have only slipped away into the next room. I am I, and you are you. Whatever we were to each other, that we still are. Call me by my old familiar name, speak to me in the easy way that you always used. Put no difference in your tone, wear no forced air of solemnity or sorrow. Laugh as we always laughed at the little jokes we enjoyed together. Play, smile, think of me, pray for me. Let my name be ever the household word that it always was, let it be spoken without effect, without the trace of a shadow on it.

Life means all that it ever meant. It is the same as it ever was; there is unbroken continuity. Why should I be out of mind because I am out of sight? I am waiting for you, for an interval, somewhere very near, just round the corner.

All is well.

*Henry Scott Holland* (1847–1918)

## Remember Me

To the living, I am gone
To the sorrowful, I will never return
To the angry, I was cheated
But to the happy, I am at peace
And to the faithful, I have never left
I cannot speak, but I can listen
I cannot be seen, but I can be heard
So as you stand upon the shore
Gazing at the beautiful sea, remember me
As you look in awe at a mighty forest
And its grand majesty, remember me
Remember me in your hearts,
In your thoughts, and the memories of the
Times we loved, the times we cried, the
Battle we fought and the times we laughed
For if you always think of me, I will
Have never gone.

*Anon.*

## 'I'm here for a short visit only'

I'm here for a short visit only
And I'd rather be loved than hated
Eternity may be lonely
When my body's disintegrated
And that which is loosely termed my soul
Goes whizzing off through the infinite
By means of some vague remote control
I'd like to think I was missed a bit.

*Noël Coward* (1899–1973)

# 'No longer mourn for me when I am dead'

No longer mourn for me when I am dead
Than you shall hear the surly sullen bell
Give warning to the world that I am fled
From this vile world, with vilest worms to dwell:
Nay, if you read this line, remember not
The hand that writ it, for I love you so
That I in your sweet thoughts would be forgot,
If thinking on me then should make you woe.
O if (I say) you look upon this verse,
When I, perhaps, compounded am with clay,
Do not so much as my poor name rehearse,
But let your love even with my life decay;
    Lest the wise world should look into your moan,
    And mock you with me after I am gone.

*William Shakespeare* (1564–1616)

## If Death is Kind

Perhaps if Death is kind, and there can be returning,
   We will come back to earth some fragrant night,
And take these lanes to find the sea, and bending
   Breathe the same honeysuckle, low and white.

We will come down at night to these resounding beaches
   And the long gentle thunder of the sea,
Here for a single hour in the wide starlight
   We shall be happy, for the dead are free.

*Sara Teasdale* (1884–1933)

## Fare Well

When I lie where shades of darkness
Shall no more assail mine eyes,
Nor the rain make lamentation
    When the wind sighs;
How will fare the world whose wonder
Was the very proof of me?
Memory fades, must the remembered
    Perishing be?

Oh, when this my dust surrenders
Hand, foot, lip, to dust again,
May these loved and loving faces
    Please other men!
May the rusting harvest hedgerow
Still the Traveller's Joy entwine,
And as happy children gather
    Posies once mine.

Look thy last on all things lovely,
Every hour. Let no night
Seal thy sense in deathly slumber
    Till to delight
Thou have paid thy utmost blessing;
Since that all things thou wouldst praise
Beauty took from those who loved them
    In other days.

*Walter de la Mare* (1873–1956)

## When I Died

I'm coming back on All Saints' Day
for your olives, old peanuts and dodgy sherry,
dirty dancing. I'll cross-dress at last
pirouette and flash, act pissed.
You'll have to look for me hard:
search for my bones in the crowd.
Or lay a pint and a pie on my grave to tempt me out
and a trail of marigolds back to the flat,
where you'll leave the door ajar
and the cushions plumped in my old armchair.

*Jo Shapcott* (1953– )

# 'Because I could not stop for Death'

Because I could not stop for Death –
He kindly stopped for me –
The Carriage held but just Ourselves –
And Immortality.

We slowly drove – He knew no haste
And I had put away
My labor and my leisure too,
For His Civility –

We passed the School, where Children strove
At Recess – in the Ring –
We passed the Fields of Gazing Grain –
We passed the Setting Sun –

Or rather – He passed us –
The Dews grew quivering and chill –
For only Gossamer, my Gown –
My Tippet – only Tulle –

We paused before a House that seemed
A Swelling of the Ground –
The Roof was scarcely visible –
The Cornice – in the Ground –

Since then – 'tis Centuries – and yet
Feels shorter then the Day
I first surmised the Horses' heads
Were toward Eternity –

*Emily Dickinson* (1830–86)

# 'I see myself now at the end of my journey'

I see myself now at the end of my journey; my toilsome days are ended. I am going to see that head which was crowned with thorns, and that face which was spit upon for me. I have formerly lived by hearsay and faith, but now I go where I shall live by sight, and shall be with Him in whose company I delight myself. I have loved to hear my Lord spoken of; and wherever I have seen the print of his shoe in the earth, there I have coveted to set my foot too. His name to me has been as a civet-box; yea, sweeter than all perfumes. His voice to me has been most sweet; and his countenance I have more desired than they that have most desired the light of the sun. His words I did use to gather for my food, and for antidotes against my faintings. He has held me, and has kept me from mine iniquities; yea, my steps hath he strengthened in his way.

Now, while he was thus in discourse, his countenance changed; his strong man bowed under him; and after he had said, 'Take me, for I come unto Thee!' he ceased to be seen of them.

But glorious it was to see how the upper region was filled with horses and chariots, with trumpeters and pipers, with singers and players on stringed instruments, to welcome the pilgrims as they went up, and followed one another in at the beautiful gate of the city.

from *The Pilgrim's Progress*, John Bunyan (1628–88)

# Requiem

Under the wide and starry sky
Dig the grave and let me lie:
Glad did I live and gladly die,
   And I laid me down with a will.

This be the verse you grave for me:
*Here he lies where he longed to be;*
*Home is the sailor, home from sea,*
   *And the hunter home from the hill.*

   *Robert Louis Stevenson* (1850–94)

## 'I thought I'd write my own obituary'

I thought I'd write my own obituary. Instead,
I wrote the blurb for when I'm risen from the dead:

Ignite the flares, connect the phones, wind all the clocks;
the sun goes rusty like a medal in its box –
collect it from the loft. Peg out the stars,
replace the bulbs of Jupiter and Mars.
A man like that takes something with him when he dies,
but he has wept the coins that rested on his eyes,
eased out the stopper from the mouthpiece of the cave,
exhumed his own white body from the grave.

Unlock the rivers, hoist the dawn and launch the sea.
Set up the skittles of the orchard and the wood again,
now everything is clear and straight and free and good
again.

*Simon Armitage* (1963– )

## Think of Me Then

On a day of rain when you sit indoors
By the fire with a book, as I loved to do,
And the storm wind roars
Think of me then.

As you walk by the shore when the sun is high
And the sea is blue, as I loved to do,
And the seagulls cry
Think of me then.

When you're skimming stones in the fading light
Choosing them smooth, as I loved to do,
And they skip out of sight
Think of me then.

When you sit in the garden in summer and keep
Watch with the night, as I loved to do
Go to sleep,
Dream of me then.

*Asa James* (1972– )

# The New Path

Now I know what is meant by death –
A leavetaking
In one way, in another
A kind of waking.

The old world almost gone
your voices ringing
in my ears like a distant echo
barely clinging.

The stones of the earth are warm
and the grass is singing
as I start down my new path
to my new beginning.

*Oscar Beynon* (1962– )

## Footprints in the Sand

One night I dreamed I was walking
Along the beach with the Lord,

Many scenes from my life flashed across the sky.
In each scene I noticed footprints in the sand.

Sometimes there were two sets of footprints.
Other times there was only one.

This bothered me because I noticed
During the low periods of my life when I was

Suffering from anguish, sorrow or defeat,
I could see only one set of footprints.

So I said to the Lord, 'You promised me,
Lord, that if I followed You,
You would walk with me always.

But I noticed during the most trying periods
Of my life there has only been
One set of prints in the sand.

Why, when I needed You most,
Have You not been there for me?'

The Lord replied,
'The times when you have seen only one set of footprints
It was then that I carried you.'

*Anon.*

## The Book

Go to that place we loved, our secret place.
Close your eyes and you'll see my face.

Play that tune, the tune we loved to hear.
Close your eyes and you'll see me clear.

Walk on a beach or climb to the top of a hill.
Close your eyes and you'll see me still.

Take a sip of wine, of dark red wine.
Close your eyes and you'll see me fine.

At night go out and look at the brightest star.
Close your eyes and you'll see me far.

On a day when the sky is blue and cold and clear,
Close your eyes and you'll see me near.

Take down a book that would have been my choice.
Open the book. Close your eyes. You'll hear my voice.

*Paul Meadows* (1969– )

## The Legacy

The song of the wind in the tree
The hang and heave of the sea
The cry of a bird on the wing
This is my legacy.

The sun on a frosting of dew
The rain when it comes on cue
The greening and the shining
I leave all this to you.

*Sarah-Jane Brooks* (1963– )

# 'A thing of beauty is a joy for ever'

A thing of beauty is a joy for ever:
Its loveliness increases; it will never
Pass into nothingness; but still will keep
A bower quiet for us, and a sleep
Full of sweet dreams, and health, and quiet breathing.
Therefore, on every morrow, are we wreathing
A flowery band to bind us to the earth,
Spite of despondence, of the inhuman dearth
Of noble natures, of the gloomy days,
Of all the unhealthy and o'er-darkened ways
Made for our searching: yes, in spite of all,
Some shape of beauty moves away the pall
From our dark spirits . . .

from *Endymion*, John Keats (1795–1821)

## When I Have Fears

When I have fears, as Keats had fears,
Of the moment I'll cease to be
I console myself with vanished years
Remembered laughter, remembered tears,
And the peace of the changing sea.

When I feel sad, as Keats felt sad,
That my life is so nearly done
It gives me comfort to dwell upon
Remembered friends who are dead and gone
And the jokes we had and the fun.

How happy they are I cannot know
But happy am I who loved them so.

*Noël Coward* (1899–1973)

## A Song of Living

Because I have loved life, I shall have no sorrow to die.
I have sent up my gladness on wings, to be lost in the blue of
   the sky.
I have run and leaped with the rain, I have taken the wind to my
   breast.
My cheek like a drowsy child to the face of the earth I have
   pressed.
Because I have loved life, I shall have no sorrow to die.

I have kissed young Love on the lips, I have heard his song to
   the end.
I have struck my hand like a seal in the loyal hand of a friend.
I have known the peace of heaven, the comfort of work done
   well.
I have longed for death in the darkness and risen alive out of
   hell.
Because I have loved life, I shall have no sorrow to die.

I give a share of my soul to the world where my course is run.
I know that another shall finish the task I must leave undone.
I know that no flower, nor flint was in vain on the path I trod.
As one looks on a face through a window, through life I have
   looked on God.
Because I have loved life, I shall have no sorrow to die.

*Amelia Josephine Burr* (1878–?)

# 'I should like to be buried in a summer forest'

I should like to be buried in a summer forest
where people go in July,
only a bus ride from the city,

I should like them to walk over me
not noticing anything but sunlight
and patches of wild strawberries –

*Here! Look under the leaves!*
I should like the child who is slowest
to end up picking the most,

and the big kids will show the little
the only way to grasp a nettle
and pick it so it doesn't sting.

I should like home-time to come
so late the bus has its lights on
and a cloud of moths hangs in their beam,

and when they are all gone
I should like to be buried in a summer forest
where the dark steps
blindfold, on cat foot-pads,
with the dawn almost touching it.

*Helen Dunmore* (1952– )

## 'I would not have a god come in'

I would not have a god come in
To shield me suddenly from sin,
And set my house of life to rights;
Nor angels with bright burning wings
Ordering my earthly thoughts and things;
Rather my own frail guttering lights
Wind blown and nearly beaten out;
Rather the terror of the nights
And long, sick groping after doubt;
Rather be lost than let my soul
Slip vaguely from my own control –
Of my own spirit let me be
In sole though feeble mastery.

*Sara Teasdale* (1884–1933)

# I've Made Out a Will

I've made out a will; I'm leaving myself
to the National Health. I'm sure they can use
the jellies and tubes and syrups and glues,
the web of nerves and veins, the loaf of brains,
an assortment of fillings and stitches and wounds,
blood – a gallon exactly of bilberry soup –
the chassis or cage or cathedral of bone;
but not the heart, they can leave that alone.

They can have the lot, the whole stock:
the loops and coils and sprockets and springs and rods,
the twines and cords and strands,
the face, the case, the cogs and the hands,

but not the pendulum, the ticker;
leave that where it stops or hangs.

*Simon Armitage* (1963– )

# Coda

There's little in taking or giving,
There's little in water or wine;
This living, this living, this living
Was never a project of mine.
Oh, hard is the struggle, and sparse is
The gain of the one at the top,
For art is a form of catharsis,
And love is a permanent flop,
And work is the province of cattle,
And rest's for a clam in a shell,
So I'm thinking of throwing the battle –
Would you kindly direct me to hell?

*Dorothy Parker* (1893–1967)

## Rest

The memories and love I leave behind
Are yours to keep
I have found my rest; I have turned my face
To the sun, and now I sleep.

*Alan Curtis* (1959– )

## *Prayer*

My Lord God, I have no idea where I am going. I do not see the road ahead of me. I cannot know for certain where it will end. Nor do I really know myself, and the fact that I think I am following your will does not mean I am actually doing so. But I believe the desire to please you does in fact please you. And I hope I have the desire in all that I am doing. I hope I will never do anything apart from that desire. And I know that if I do this you will lead me by the right road though I may know nothing about it. Therefore I will trust you always though I may seem to be lost and in the shadow of death. I will not fear for you are ever with me and you will never leave me to face my troubles alone.

*Thomas Merton* (1915–68)

*A tiny lamp has gone out in my tent . . .*

God, give us grace to accept with serenity the things that cannot
   be changed,
Courage to change the things that should be changed,
And the wisdom to distinguish the one from the other.

'The Serenity Prayer', Reinhold Niebuhr (1892–1971)

## 'You must not shut the night inside you'

You must not shut the night inside you,
But endlessly in light the dark immerse.
A tiny lamp has gone out in my tent –
I bless the flame that warms the universe.

from *Kindertotenlieder* (*Songs of the
Death of Children*),
Friedrich Rückert (1788–1866)

## Prayer for the Little Daughter between Death and Burial

Now you are standing face to face with the clear light
believe in it
Now you have gone back into where air comes from
hold fast to it
Now you have climbed to the top of the topless tower
and there are no stairs down
and the only way is flight past the edge of the world
do not remember us

Like the new moon in the sky of the shortest day
you came to us
as the candles burnt with a steady light behind misty windows
you whispered to us
as the singers moved behind doors of un-attainable rooms
you burst in on us
Lady of the shortest day, silent upon the threshold
carrying green branches

Lady of the crown of light going into clear light
be safe on your journey
Bright lady of the dark day, who pushed back the darkness
say nothing to us
as we plod through the frozen field
going from somewhere to somewhere
do not speak to us
as we stand at the centre of the frozen lake
and trees of cloud stand over us
forget us

When we come to you we shall find you
who have seen Persephone
you whom our mothers called Lady of the city
will welcome us with tapers, and believe in us
When small harsh birds bubble and pump in our nude trees
and water will rush and gush through the slippery street
and two skies will look at each other
one of air and one below
of water
you will rest with us, and of us:
Lady of the shortest day
watch over our daughter
whom we commit to the grass

*Diana Scott* (1947– )

## Epitaph on a Child

Here, freed from pain, secure from misery, lies
A child, the darling of his parents' eyes:
A gentler Lamb ne'er sported on the plain,
A fairer flower will never bloom again:
Few were the days allotted to his breath;
Now let him sleep in peace his night of death.

*Thomas Gray* (1716–71)

## On the Death of a Child

The greatest griefs shall find themselves inside the smallest cage.
It's only then that we can hope to tame their rage,

The monsters we must live with. For it will not do
To hiss humanity because one human threw
Us out of heart and home. Or part

At odds with life because one baby failed to live.
Indeed, as little as its subject, is the wreath we give –

The big words fail to fit. Like giant boxes
Round small bodies. Taking up improper room,
Where so much withering is, and so much bloom.

*D. J. Enright* (1920–2002)

# Four Candles

The first candle represents our grief.
The pain of losing you is intense
It reminds us of the depth of our love for you.

The second candle represents our courage.
To confront our sorrow,
To comfort each other,
To change our lives.

This third candle we light in your memory.
For the times we laughed,
The times we cried,
The times we were angry with each other,
The silly things you did,
The caring and joy you gave us.

This fourth candle we light for our love.
We light this candle that your light will always shine
As we enter this sad time and share this day of remembrance
With family and friends.
We cherish the special place in our hearts
That will always be reserved for you.

We thank you for the gift
Your living brought to each of us.

*Anon.*

## Too Soon

This was a life
That had hardly begun
No time to find
Your place in the sun
No time to do
All you could have done
But we loved you enough for a lifetime.

No time to enjoy
The world and its wealth
No time to take life
Down off the shelf
No time to sing
The song of yourself
Though you had enough love for a lifetime.

Those who live long
Endure sadness and tears
But you'll never suffer
The sorrowing years:
No betrayal, no anger,
No hatred, no fears,
Just love – only love – in your lifetime.

*Mary Yarnall* (1955– )

# Requiescat

Tread lightly, she is near
    Under the snow,
Speak gently, she can hear
    The daisies grow.

All her bright golden hair
    Tarnished with rust,
She that was young and fair
    Fallen to dust.

Lily-like, white as snow,
    She hardly knew
She was a woman, so
    Sweetly she grew.

Coffin-board, heavy stone,
    Lie on her breast,
I vex my heart alone,
    She is at rest.

Peace, Peace, she cannot hear
    Lyre or sonnet,
All my life's buried here,
    Heap earth upon it.

*Oscar Wilde* (1854–1900)

## 'Promise you won't forget about me, ever'

Then, suddenly again, Christopher Robin, who was still looking at the world with his chin in his hands, called out 'Pooh!'

'Yes?' said Pooh.

'When I'm – when – Pooh!'

'Yes, Christopher Robin?'

'I'm not going to do Nothing any more.'

'Never again?'

'Well, not so much. They don't let you.'

Pooh waited for him to go on, but he was silent again.

'Yes, Christopher Robin?' said Pooh helpfully.

'Pooh, when I'm – *you* know – when I'm *not* doing Nothing, will you come up here sometimes?'

'Just Me?'

'Yes, Pooh.'

'Will you be here too?'

'Yes, Pooh, I will be really. I *promise* I will be, Pooh.'

'That's good,' said Pooh.

'Pooh, *promise* you won't forget about me, ever. Not even when I'm a hundred.'

Pooh thought for a little.

'How old shall *I* be then?'

'Ninety-nine.'

Pooh nodded.

'I promise,' he said.

Still with his eyes on the world Christopher Robin put out a hand and felt for Pooh's paw.

'Pooh,' said Christopher Robin earnestly, 'if I – if I'm not quite –' he stopped and tried again – 'Pooh, *whatever* happens you *will* understand, won't you?'

'Understand what?'

'Oh, nothing.' He laughed and jumped to his feet. 'Come on!'

'Where?' said Pooh.

'Anywhere,' said Christopher Robin.

So they went off together. But wherever they go, and whatever happens to them on the way, in that enchanted place on the top of the Forest a little boy and his Bear will always be playing.

from *The House at Pooh Corner*, A. A. Milne (1882–1956)

*He was my North, my South,
my East and West . . .*

A thousand years you said,
as our hearts melted.
I look at the hand that you held,
and the ache is hard to bear.

Lady Heguri
(mid–late eighth century),
translated from the Japanese by
Geoffrey Bownas and
Anthony Thwaite

## Funeral Blues

Stop all the clocks, cut off the telephone,
Prevent the dog from barking with a juicy bone,
Silence the pianos and with muffled drum
Bring out the coffin, let the mourners come.

Let aeroplanes circle moaning overhead
Scribbling on the sky the message He Is Dead,
Put crêpe bows round the white necks of the public doves,
Let the traffic policemen wear black cotton gloves.

He was my North, my South, my East and West,
My working week and my Sunday rest,
My noon, my midnight, my talk, my song;
I thought that love would last for ever: I was wrong.

The stars are not wanted now; put out every one;
Pack up the moon and dismantle the sun;
Pour away the ocean and sweep up the wood;
For nothing now can ever come to any good.

*W. H. Auden* (1907–73)

## 'Music, when soft voices die'

Music, when soft voices die,
Vibrates in the memory;
Odours, when sweet violets sicken,
Live within the sense they quicken.

Rose leaves, when the rose is dead,
Are heap'd for the belovèd's bed;
And so thy thoughts, when thou art gone,
Love itself shall slumber on.

*Percy Bysshe Shelley* (1792–1822)

## 'As birds are fitted to the boughs'

As birds are fitted to the boughs
That blossom on the tree
And whisper when the south wind blows –
So was my love to me.

And still she blossoms in my mind
And whispers softly, though
The clouds are fitted to the wind,
The wind is to the snow.

*Louis Simpson* (1923– )

# Farewell, Sweet Dust

Now I have lost you, I must scatter
All of you on the air henceforth;
Not that to me it can ever matter
But it's only fair to the rest of earth.

Now especially, when it is winter
And the sun's not half as bright as he was,
Who wouldn't be glad to find a splinter
That once was you, in the frozen grass?

Snowflakes, too, will be softer feathered,
Clouds, perhaps, will be whiter plumed;
Rain, whose brilliance you caught and gathered,
Purer silver have reassumed.

Farewell, sweet dust; I never was a miser:
Once, for a minute, I made you mine:
Now you are gone, I am none the wiser
But the leaves of the willow are as bright as wine.

*Elinor Wylie* (1885–1928)

# Echo

Come to me in the silence of the night;
   Come in the speaking silence of a dream;
Come with soft rounded cheeks and eyes as bright
   As sunlight on a stream;
     Come back in tears,
O memory, hope, love of finished years.

Oh dream how sweet, too sweet, too bitter sweet,
   Whose wakening should have been in Paradise,
Where souls brimfull of love abide and meet;
   Where thirsting longing eyes
     Watch the slow door
That opening, letting in, lets out no more.

Yet come to me in dreams, that I may live
   My very life again though cold in death:
Come back to me in dreams, that I may give
   Pulse for pulse, breath for breath:
     Speak low, lean low,
As long ago, my love, how long ago!

*Christina Rossetti* (1830–94)

## The Kaleidoscope

To climb these stairs again, bearing a tray,
Might be to find you pillowed with your books,
Your inventories listing gowns and frocks
As if preparing for a holiday.
Or, turning from the landing, I might find
My presence watched through your kaleidoscope,
A symmetry of husbands, each redesigned
In lovely forms of foresight, prayer and hope.
I climb these stairs a dozen times a day
And, by that open door, wait, looking in
At where you died. My hands become a tray
Offering me, my flesh, my soul, my skin.
Grief wrongs us so. I stand, and wait, and cry
For the absurd forgiveness, not knowing why.

*Douglas Dunn* (1942– )

## Verses Written on Her Deathbed at Bath to Her Husband in London

Thou who dost all my worldly thoughts employ,
Thou pleasing source of all my earthly joy,
Thou tenderest husband and thou dearest friend,
To thee this first, this last adieu I send.
At length the conqueror Death asserts his right,
And will for ever veil me from thy sight.
He woos me to him with a cheerful grace,
And not one terror clouds his meagre face.
He promises a lasting rest from pain,
And shows that all life's fleeting joys are vain.
Th'eternal scenes of Heaven he sets in view,
And tells me that no other joys are true.
But love, fond love, would yet resist his power,
Would fain awhile defer the parting hour.
He brings thy mourning image to mine eyes,
And would obstruct my journey to the skies.
But say, thou dearest, thou unwearied friend,
Say, shouldst thou grieve to see my sorrows end?
Thou knowst a painful pilgrimage I've pass'd,
And shouldst thou grieve that rest is come at last?
Rather rejoice to see me shake off life,
And die as I have lived, thy faithful wife.

*Mary Monk* (?1677–1715)

# A Widow's Hymn

How near me came the hand of Death,
  When at my side he struck my dear,
And took away that precious breath
  Which quicken'd my belovèd peer!
    How helpless am I thereby made!
    By day how grieved, by night how sad!
And now my life's delight is gone,
– Alas! how am I left alone!

The voice which I did more esteem
  Than music in her sweetest key,
Those eyes which unto me did seem
  More comfortable than the day;
    Those now by me, as they have been,
    Shall never more be heard or seen;
But what I once enjoy'd in them
Shall seem hereafter as a dream.

Lord! keep me faithful to the trust
  Which my dear spouse reposed in me:
To him now dead preserve me just
  In all that should performèd be!
    For though our being man and wife
    Extendeth only to this life,
Yet neither life nor death should end
The being of a faithful friend.

*George Wither* (1588–1667)

## 'Time does not bring relief'

Time does not bring relief; you all have lied
Who told me time would ease me of my pain!
I miss him in the weeping of the rain;
I want him at the shrinking of the tide;
The old snows melt from every mountain-side,
And last year's leaves are smoke in every lane;
But last year's bitter loving must remain
Heaped on my heart, and my old thoughts abide!

There are a hundred places where I fear
To go, – so with his memory they brim!
And entering with relief some quiet place
Where never fell his foot or shone his face
I say, 'There is no memory of him here!'
And so stand stricken, so remembering him.

*Edna St Vincent Millay* (1892–1950)

# Tomorrows

After this day has darkened and gone
And I wake to the rest of my life
I shall think of the times and the places we saw
When we were husband and wife.

And I know I shall visit those places we loved
And walk by the fields and the sea
Where you and I spent our happiest hours
And somehow you'll be there with me.

If I go through the woods to the top of the hill
Or run barefoot over the sand
I shall hear your voice in the wind, my love,
And feel the touch of your hand.

And people who see me on my own
As they pass me on the track
Might wonder why, if I'm really alone,
I pause sometimes and look back

To where the roadside trees are blurred
By the early evening mist;
I'll be waiting for you to catch up, my love,
From where you've stopped to rest.

And though people will find many ways to be kind
They will never understand
How I hear your voice in the sigh of the wind
And feel the touch of your hand.

*Simon Bridges* (1965– )

## 'Never more will the wind'

Never more will the wind
cherish you again,
never more will the rain.

Never more
shall we find you bright
in the snow and wind.

The snow is melted,
the snow is gone,
and you are flown:

Like a bird out of our hand,
like a light out of our heart,
you are gone.

*H. D.* (1886–1961)

## Marriage and Death

We are not dovetailed but opened to each other
So that our edges blur, and to and fro
A little wind-borne trade plies, filtering over,
Bartering our atoms when fair breezes blow.

Though, not like waters met and inter-running,
Our peoples dwell each under different sky,
Here at high, unsurveyed, dissolving frontiers
We cannot prove: 'This is you, this is I.'

Oh now in you, no more in myself only
And God, I partly live, and seem to have died,
So given up, entered and entering wholly
(To cross the threshold is to be inside),

And wonder if at last, each through each far dispersed,
We shall die easily who loved this dying first.

*E. J. Scovell* (1907–99)

## Inseparable

When thou and I are dead, my dear,
  The earth above us lain;
When we no more in autumn hear
  The fall of leaves and rain,
Or round the snow-enshrouded year
  The midnight winds complain;

When we no more in green mid-spring,
  Its sights and sounds may mind, –
The warm wet leaves set quivering
  With touches of the wind,
The birds at morn, and birds that sing
  When day is left behind;

When, over all, the moonlight lies,
  Intensely bright and still;
When some meandering brooklet sighs
  At parting from its hill,
And scents from voiceless gardens rise,
  The peaceful air to fill;

When we no more through summer light
  The deep dim woods discern,
Nor hear the nightingales at night,
  In vehement singing, yearn
To stars and moon, that dumb and bright,
  In nightly vigil burn;

When smiles and hopes and joys and fears
  And words that lovers say,
And sighs of love, and passionate tears
  Are lost to us, for aye, –

What thing of all our love appears,
 In cold and coffin'd clay?

When all their kisses, sweet and close,
 Our lips shall quite forget;
When, where the day upon us rose,
 The day shall rise and set,
While we for love's sublime repose,
 Shall have not one regret, –

Oh, this true comfort is, I think,
 That, be death near or far,
When we have crossed the fatal brink,
 And found nor moon nor star,
We know not, when in death we sink,
 The lifeless things we are.

Yet one thought is, I deem, more kind,
 That when we sleep so well,
On memories that we leave behind
 When kindred souls shall dwell,
My name to thine in words they'll bind
 Of love inseparable.

*Philip Bourke Marston* (1850–87)

## 'Dear gentle soul, who went so soon away'

Dear gentle soul, who went so soon away
Departing from this life in discontent,
Repose in that far sky to which you went
While on this earth I linger in dismay.
In the ethereal seat where you must be,
If you consent to memories of our sphere,
Recall the love which, burning pure and clear,
So often in my eyes you used to see!
If then, in the incurable, long anguish
Of having lost you, as I pine and languish,
You see some merit – do this favour for me:
And to the God who cut your life short, pray
That he as early to your sight restore me
As from my own he swept you far away.

*Luis de Camoëns* (1527–80),
translated from the Portuguese by
Roy Campbell

## *In Memoriam E. S.*

Ah most unreliable of all women of grace
in the breathless hurry of your leave-taking
you forgot – you forgot for ever – our last embrace.

*George Barker* (1913–91)

*Worn features of ancestral mould . . .*

To live in the hearts of those we leave behind is not to die.

inscription on a headstone in
Lytham St Annes, Lancashire

## *Highland Graveyard*

Today a fine old face has gone under the soil;
For generations past women hereabouts have borne
Her same name and stamp of feature.
Her brief identity was not her own
But theirs who formed and sent her out
To wear the proud bones of her clan, and live its story,
Who now receive back into the ground
Worn features of ancestral mould.

A dry-stone wall bounds off the dislimned clay
Of many an old face forgotten and young face gone
From boundless nature, sea and sky.
A wind-withered escalonia like a song
Of ancient tenderness lives on
Some woman's living fingers set as shelter for the dead, to tell
In evergreen unwritten leaves,
In scent of leaves in western rain
That one remembered who is herself forgotten.

Many songs they knew who now are silent.
Into their memories the dead are gone
Who haunt the living in an ancient tongue
Sung by old voices to the young,
Telling of sea and isles, of boat and byre and glen;
And from their music the living are reborn
Into a remembered land,
To call ancestral memories home
And all that ancient grief and love our own.

*Kathleen Raine* (1908–2003)

# 'Another and another and another'

Another and another and another
And still another sunset and sunrise,
The same yet different, different yet the same,
Seen by me now in my declining years
As in my early childhood, youth and manhood;
And by my parents and my parents' parents,
And by the parents of my parents' parents,
And by their parents counted back for ever,
Seen, all their lives long, even as now by me;
And by my children and my children's children
And by the children of my children's children
And by their children counted on for ever
Still to be seen as even now seen by me;
Clear and bright sometimes, sometimes dark and clouded
But still the same sunsetting and sunrise;
The same for ever to the never ending
Line of observers, to the same observer
Through all the changes of his life the same:
Sunsetting and sunrising and sunsetting,
And then again sunrising and sunsetting,
Sunrising and sunsetting evermore.

*James Henry* (1798–1876)

## 'Fear no more the heat o' the sun'

Fear no more the heat o' the sun,
   Nor the furious winter's rages,
Thou thy worldly task hast done
   Home art gone and ta'en thy wages.
Golden lads and girls all must,
As chimney-sweepers, come to dust.

Fear no more the frown o' the great,
   Thou art past the tyrant's stroke
Care no more to clothe and eat,
   To thee the reed is as the oak:
The sceptre, learning, physic, must
All follow this, and come to dust.

Fear no more the lightning-flash.
   Nor the all-dreaded thunder-stone.
Fear not slander, censure rash.
   Thou hast finish'd joy and moan.
All lovers young, all lovers must
Consign to thee, and come to dust.

No exorcizer harm thee!
Nor no witchcraft charm thee!
Ghost unlaid forbear thee!
Nothing ill come near thee!
Quiet consummation have,
And renownèd be thy grave!

     from *Cymbeline* (IV. ii),
William Shakespeare (1564–1616)

## 'By ways remote and distant waters sped'

By ways remote and distant waters sped,
Brother, to thy sad grave-side am I come,
That I may give the last gifts to the dead,
And vainly parley with thine ashes dumb:
Since she who now bestows and now denies
Hath ta'en thee, hapless brother, from mine eyes.
But lo! these gifts, the heirlooms of past years,
Are made sad things to grace thy coffin shell,
Take them, all drenched with a brother's tears,
And, brother, for all time, hail and farewell!

*Catullus* (?84–?54 BC), translated from the Latin
by Aubrey Beardsley

## 'Like as the waves make towards the pebbled shore'

Like as the waves make towards the pebbled shore,
So do our minutes hasten to their end,
Each changing place with that which goes before,
In sequent toil all forwards do contend.
Nativity, once in the main of light,
Crawls to maturity, wherewith being crown'd,
Crooked eclipses 'gainst his glory fight,
And Time, that gave, doth now his gift confound.
Time doth transfix the flourish set on youth,
And delves the parallels in beauty's brow;
Feeds on the rarities of nature's truth,
And nothing stands but for his scythe to mow.
     And yet to times in hope my verse shall stand,
     Praising thy worth, despite his cruel hand.

*William Shakespeare* (1564–1616)

## *Elegy*

On the day of your death there were leaves drifting
Down to English lawns as season
Drifted into season, winter coming; and rooks were pouring
Across the sky, thick as the falling leaves and giving
Their hoarse Kyrie Eleison,
The best of the day now fading, you yourself fading
For no good reason, it seemed, for no good reason.

And in every part of the garden dark doors closing.

*David Harsent* (1942– )

# I Wish You Enough

A father and daughter were saying goodbye at an airport. Her plane had been called. I was sitting near by and heard him say, 'I wish you enough.' She said, 'Daddy, your love and care in my life have been more than enough.' They kissed goodbye and she added: 'I wish you enough too.' Then she left to board her plane.

As he watched her go, he was crying. I asked him if there was anything I could do. He shook his head, but smiled and thanked me. 'I am saying goodbye to my daughter for ever. I am old and I have an illness that will soon take its toll. My daughter lives a long way away. She has work to do, and so have I. We both know that when she returns it will be for my funeral.'

I said, 'I heard you say, "I wish you enough"; what did you mean?' He smiled again. 'It's a saying in our family, passed down through generations. I don't quite know where it came from, but it's precious to us.' Then he closed his eyes a moment and spoke it from memory:

*I wish you enough sun to keep your outlook bright. I wish you enough rain to appreciate the sun. I wish you enough happiness to keep your spirit strong. I wish you enough pain to make life's joys seem precious. I wish you enough luck to satisfy your needs. I wish you enough loss to appreciate what you keep. I wish you enough hellos to help you through the final goodbye.*

When he left, I wrote the words down. Now I have them by heart. And from my heart, I say:

*My friends, I wish you enough.*

*Anon.*

## While I Slept

While I slept, while I slept and the night grew colder
She would come to my room, stepping softly
And draw a blanket about my shoulder
While I slept.

While I slept, while I slept in the dark, still heat
She would come to my bedside, stepping coolly
And smooth the twisted, troubled sheet
While I slept.

Now she sleeps, sleeps under quiet rain
While nights grow warm or nights grow colder.
And I wake, and sleep, and wake again
While she sleeps.

*Robert Francis* (1901–87)

# 'Do not go gentle into that good night'

Do not go gentle into that good night,
Old age should burn and rave at close of day;
Rage, rage against the dying of the light.

Though wise men at their end know dark is right,
Because their words have forked no lightning they
Do not go gentle into that good night.

Good men, the last wave by, crying how bright
Their frail deeds might have danced in a green bay,
Rage, rage against the dying of the light.

Wild men who caught and sang the sun in flight,
And learn, too late, they grieved it on its way.
Do not go gentle into that good night.

Grave men, near death, who see with blinding sight
Blind eyes could blaze like meteors and be gay,
Rage, rage against the dying of the light.

And you, my father, there on the sad height,
Curse, bless, me now with your fierce tears, I pray.
Do not go gentle into that good night.
Rage, rage against the dying of the light.

*Dylan Thomas* (1914–53)

# Coat

Sometimes I have wanted
to throw you off
like a heavy coat.

Sometimes I have said
you would not let me
breathe or move.

But now that I am free
to choose light clothes
or none at all

I feel the cold
and all the time I think
how warm it used to be.

*Vicki Feaver* (1943– )

## 'The rooms and days we wandered through'

The rooms and days we wandered through
Shrink in my mind to one – there you
Lie quite absorbed by peace – the calm
Which life could not provide is balm
In death. Unseen by me, you look
Past bed and stairs and half-read book
Eternally upon your home,
The end of pain, the left alone.
I have no friend, or intercessor,
No psychopomp or true confessor
But only you who know my heart
In every cramped and devious part –
Then take my hand and lead me out,
The sky is overcast by doubt,
The time has come, I listen for
Your words of comfort at the door,
O guide me through the shoals of fear –
'Fürchte dich nicht, ich bin bei dir.'

From *An Exequy*, Peter Porter (1929– )

## The Friend

In a circle of friends, the one who dies first
is the friend you will never forget:
this is the death that unhinges you
from the trappings of everyday life
and makes you – suddenly – absurdly grateful
for each new breath – beginning with this one.

This is the death that could break you apart
in every way possible; that persuades you –
in memory of that friend – to turn away
from whatever refuses to speak to your heart
from whatever threatens to numb your soul
from whatever it is that revels in death.

Yet this, too, is the friend you need by your side.
Listen. Together they urge you: *Live your life*.

*Alice Kavounas* (1945– )

## 'You can shed tears that she is gone'

You can shed tears that she is gone
or you can smile because she has lived.

You can close your eyes and pray that she'll come back
or you can open your eyes and see all she's left.

Your heart can be empty because you can't see her
or you can be full of the love you shared.

You can turn your back on tomorrow and live yesterday
or you can be happy for tomorrow because of yesterday.

You can remember her and only that she's gone
or you can cherish her memory and let it live on.

You can cry and close your mind, be empty and turn your back
or you can do what she'd want: smile, open your eyes
love and go on.

*Anon.*

## Inside Our Dreams

Where do people go to when they die?
Somewhere down below or in the sky?
'I can't be sure,' said Grandad, 'but it seems
They simply set up home inside our dreams.'

*Jeanne Willis* (1959– )

## Traditional Gaelic Blessing

May the road rise up to meet you.
May the wind be always at your back.
May the sun shine warm upon your face;
the rains fall soft upon your fields and until we meet again,
may God hold you in the palm of His hand.

*To every thing there is a season . . .*

When we die, the wind blows away our footprints and that is the end
of us.

Kalahari bushmen

## 'To every thing there is a season'

To every thing there is a season, and a time to every purpose
under the heaven:
A time to be born, and a time to die; a time to plant, and a time
to pluck up that which is planted:
A time to kill, and a time to heal; a time to break down, and a
time to build up;
A time to weep, and a time to laugh; a time to mourn, and a time
to dance;
A time to cast away stones, and a time to gather stones together;
a time to embrace, and a time to refrain from embracing;
A time to get, and a time to lose; a time to keep, and a time to
cast away;
A time to rend, and a time to sew; a time to keep silence, and a
time to speak;
A time to love, and a time to hate; a time of war, and a time of
peace.

Ecclesiastes 3: 1–8 (King James version)

## 'Our revels now are ended'

Our revels now are ended. These our actors,
As I foretold you, were all spirits, and
Are melted into air, into thin air:
And, like the baseless fabric of this vision,
The cloud-capp'd towers, the gorgeous palaces,
The solemn temples, the great globe itself,
Yea, all which it inherit, shall dissolve,
And, like this insubstantial pageant faded,
Leave not a rack behind. We are such stuff
As dreams are made on; and our little life
Is rounded with a sleep.

from *The Tempest* (IV.i),
William Shakespeare (1564–1616)

# *So Many Different Lengths of Time*

*Cuánto vive el hombre, por fin? Vive mil días o uno solo?*
*Una semana o varios siglos? Por cuánto tiempo muere el hombre?*
*Qué quiere decir 'Para Siempre'?*
*Preocupado por este asunto me dediqué a aclarar las cosas.*

*Pablo Neruda*

How long is a man's life, finally?
Is it a thousand days, or only one?
One week, or a few centuries?
How long does a man's death last?
And what do we mean when we say, 'gone forever'?

Adrift in such preoccupations, we seek clarification.
We can go to the philosophers,
but they will grow tired of our questions.
We can go to the priests and the rabbis,
but they might be too busy with administrations.

So, how long does a man live, finally?
And how much does he live while he lives?
We fret, and ask so many questions –
then when it comes to us
the answer is so simple.

A man lives for as long as we carry him inside us,
for as long as we carry the harvest of his dreams,
for as long as we ourselves live,
holding memories in common, a man lives.

His lover will carry his man's scent, his touch;
his children will carry the weight of his love.
One friend will carry his arguments,
another will hum his favourite tunes,
another will still share his terrors.

And the days will pass with baffled faces,
then the weeks, then the months,
then there will be a day when no question is asked,
and the knots of grief will loosen in the stomach,
and the puffed faces will calm.
And on that day he will not have ceased,
but will have ceased to be separated by death.
How long does a man live, finally?

A man lives so many different lengths of time.

*Brian Patten* (1946– )

## 'Come, fill the Cup'

### VII

Come, fill the Cup, and in the fire of Spring
Your Winter-garment of Repentance fling:
   The Bird of Time has but a little way
To flutter – and the Bird is on the Wing.

   . . .

### XXI

Ah, my Belovéd, fill the Cup that clears
TO-DAY of past Regrets and future Fears:
   To-morrow! – why, To-morrow I may be
Myself with Yesterday's Sev'n thousand Years.

### XXII

For some we loved, the loveliest and the best
That from his Vintage rolling Time hath prest,
   Have drunk their Cup a Round or two before,
And one by one crept silently to rest.

### XXIII

And we, that now make merry in the Room
They left, and Summer dresses in new bloom,
   Ourselves must we beneath the Couch of Earth
Descend – ourselves to make a Couch – for whom?

### XXIV

Ah, make the most of what we yet may spend,
Before we too into the Dust descend;
   Dust into Dust, and under Dust, to lie,
Sans Wine, sans Song, sans Singer, and – sans End!

   . . .

### LXVIII

We are no other than a moving row
Of Magic Shadow-shapes that come and go
  Round with the Sun-illumin'd Lantern held
In Midnight by the Master of the Show;

### LXIX

But helpless Pieces of the Game He plays
Upon this Chequer-board of Nights and Days;
  Hither and thither moves, and checks, and slays,
And one by one back in the Closet lays.

### LXX

The Ball no question makes of Ayes and Noes,
But Here or There as strikes the Player goes;
  And He that toss'd you down into the field,
He knows about it all – HE knows – HE knows!

### LXXI

The Moving Finger writes; and, having writ,
Moves on: nor all your Piety nor Wit
  Shall lure it back to cancel half a Line,
Nor all your Tears wash out a Word of it.

### LXXII

And that inverted Bowl they call the Sky,
Whereunder crawling coop'd we live and die,
  Lift not your hands to It for help – for It
As impotently moves as you or I.

from *The Rubáiyát of Omar Khayyám*,
Omar Khayyám (*c.* 1048–1131), translated from
the Farsi by Edward FitzGerald

# 'Remember now thy Creator in the days of thy youth'

Remember now thy Creator in the days of thy youth, while the evil days come not, nor the years draw nigh, when thou shalt say, I have no pleasure in them.

While the sun, or the light, or the moon, or the stars, be not darkened, nor the clouds return after the rain.

In the day when the keepers of the house shall tremble, and the strong men shall bow themselves, and the grinders cease because they are few, and those that look out of the windows be darkened.

And the doors shall be shut in the streets, when the sound of the grinding is low, and he shall rise up at the voice of the bird, and all the daughters of music shall be brought low.

Also they shall be afraid of that which is high, and fears shall be in the way, and the almond tree shall flourish and the grasshopper shall be a burden, and desire shall fail: because man goeth to his long home, and the mourners go about the streets.

Or ever the silver cord be loosed, or the golden bowl be broken, or the pitcher be broken at the fountain, or the wheel broken at the cistern.

Then shall the dust return to the earth as it was: and the spirit shall return unto God who gave it.

Ecclesiastes 12: 1–7 (King James version)

## 'Though I speak with the tongues of men and of angels'

Though I speak with the tongues of men and of angels, and have not love, I am become as sounding brass, or a tinkling cymbal. And though I have the gift of prophecy, and understand all mysteries, and all knowledge; and though I have all faith, so that I could remove mountains, and I have not love, I am nothing.

And though I bestow all my goods to feed the poor, and though I give my body to be burned, and have not love, it profiteth me nothing. Love suffereth, and is kind; love envieth not; love vaunteth not itself, is not puffed up, doth not behave itself unseemly, seeketh not her own, is not easily provoked, thinketh no evil, rejoiceth not in iniquity, but rejoiceth in truth; beareth all things, believeth all things, hopeth all things, endureth all things.

Love never faileth, but whether there be prophecies, they shall fail; whether there be tongues, they shall cease; whether there be knowledge, it shall vanish away. For we know in part, and we prophesy in part. But when that which is perfect is come, then that which is in part shall be done away.

When I was a child, I spake as a child, I understood as a child, I thought as a child: but when I became a man, I put away childish things. For now we see through a glass darkly; but then face to face. Now I know in part; but then shall I know even as also I am known. And now abideth faith, hope, love, these three; but the greatest of these is love.

I Corinthians 13 (New King James version, 1982)

## 'Death be not proud'

Death be not proud, though some have called thee
Mighty and dreadful, for, thou art not so,
For, those, whom thou think'st, thou dost overthrow,
Die not, poor death, nor yet canst thou kill me.
From rest and sleep, which but thy pictures be,
Much pleasure, then from thee, much more must flow,
And soonest our best men with thee do go,
Rest of their bones, and soul's delivery.
Thou art slave to Fate, Chance, kings, and desperate men,
And dost with poison, war, and sickness dwell,
And poppy, or charms can make us sleep as well,
And better than thy stroke: why swell'st thou then?
One short sleep past, we wake eternally,
And death shall be no more; death, thou shalt die.

*John Donne* (1572–1631)

## 'Home is where one starts from'

Home is where one starts from. As we grow older
The world becomes stranger, the pattern more complicated
Of dead and living. Not the intense moment
Isolated, with no before and after,
But a lifetime burning in every moment
And not the lifetime of one man only
But of old stones that cannot be deciphered.
There is a time for the evening under starlight,
A time for the evening under lamplight
(The evening with the photograph album).
Love is most nearly itself
When here and now cease to matter.
Old men ought to be explorers
Here or there does not matter
We must be still and still moving
Into another intensity
For a further union, a deeper communion
Through the dark cold and the empty desolation,
The wave cry, the wind cry, the vast waters
Of the petrel and the porpoise. In my end is my beginning.

from 'East Coker', *Four Quartets*, T. S. Eliot (1888–1965)

# Dirge without Music

I am not resigned to the shutting away of loving hearts in the
    hard ground.
So it is, and so it will be, for so it has been, time out of mind:
Into the darkness they go, the wise and the lovely. Crowned
With lilies and with laurel they go; but I am not resigned.

Lovers and thinkers, into the earth with you.
Be one with the dull, the indiscriminate dust.
A fragment of what you felt, of what you knew,
A formula, a phrase remains, – but the best is lost.

The answers quick and keen, the honest look, the laughter, the
    love, –
They are gone. They are gone to feed the roses. Elegant and
    curled
Is the blossom. Fragrant is the blossom. I know. But I do not
    approve.
More precious was the light in your eyes than all the roses in the
    world.

Down, down, down into the darkness of the grave
Gently they go, the beautiful, the tender, the kind;
Gently they go, the intelligent, the witty, the brave
I know. But I do not approve. And I am not resigned.

*Edna St Vincent Millay* (1892–1950)

## 'don't tell me that I mourn too much'

don't tell me that I mourn too much
and I won't tell you that you mourn too much
don't tell me that I mourn too little
and I won't tell you that you mourn too little
don't tell me that I mourn in the wrong place
and I won't tell you that you mourn in the wrong place
don't tell me that I mourn at the wrong time
and I won't tell you that you mourn at the wrong time
don't tell me that I mourn in the wrong way
and I won't tell you that you mourn in the wrong way

I may get it wrong, I will get it wrong, I have got it wrong
but don't tell me

*Michael Rosen* (1946– )

## All Things Pass

All things pass
A sunrise does not last all morning
All things pass
A cloudburst does not last all day
All things pass
Nor a sunset all night
All things pass
What always changes?

Earth . . . sky . . . thunder . . .
mountain . . . water . . .
wind . . . fire . . . lake . . .

These change
And if these do not last

Do man's visions last?
Do man's illusions?

Take things as they come
All things pass

    from the *Tao Te Ching*, Lao-Tzu
    (6th century BC), translated from
    the Chinese by Timothy Leary

## Earth

Let the day grow on you upward
through your feet,
the vegetal knuckles,

to your knees of stone,
until by evening you are a black tree;
feel, with evening,

the swifts thicken your hair,
the new moon rising out of your forehead,
and the moonlit veins of silver

running from your armpits
like rivulets under white leaves.
Sleep, as ants

cross over our eyelids.
You have never possessed anything
as deeply as this.

This is all you have owned
from the first outcry
through forever;

you can never be dispossessed.

*Derek Walcott* (1930– )

# On Death

Then Almitra spoke, saying, We would ask now of Death.

And he said:

You would know the secret of death.

But how shall you find it unless you seek it in the heart of life?

The owl whose night-bound eyes are blind unto the day cannot
unveil the mystery of light.

If you would indeed behold the spirit of death, open your heart
wide unto the body of life.

For life and death are one, even as the river and the sea are one.

In the depth of your hopes and desires lies your silent
knowledge of the beyond;

And like seeds dreaming beneath the snow your heart dreams of
spring.

Trust the dreams, for in them is hidden the gate to eternity.

Your fear of death is but the trembling of the shepherd when he
stands before the king whose hand is to be laid upon him in
honour.

Is the shepherd not joyful beneath his trembling, that he shall
wear the mark of the king?

Yet is he not more mindful of his trembling?

For what is it to die but to stand naked in the wind and melt into
the sun?

And what is it to cease breathing, but to free the breath from its
restless tides, that it may rise and expand and seek God
unencumbered?

Only when you drink from the river of silence shall you indeed
sing.

And when you have reached the mountain-top, then you shall
   begin to climb.
And when the earth shall claim your limbs, then shall you truly
   dance.

from *The Prophet*, Kahlil Gibran (1883–1931)

# Gone from My Sight

I am standing upon the seashore.
A ship at my side spreads her white
sails to the morning breeze and starts
for the blue ocean.

She is an object of beauty and strength.
I stand and watch her until at length
she hangs like a speck of white cloud
just where the sea and sky come
to mingle with each other.

Then, someone at my side says:
'There, she is gone!'

'Gone where?'
Gone from my sight. That is all.
She is just as large in mast and hull
and spar as she was when she left my side
and she is just as able to bear her
load of living freight to her destined port.
Her diminished size is in me, not in her.

And just at the moment when someone
at my side says, 'There, she is gone!'
there are other eyes watching her coming,
and other voices ready to take up the glad
shout:
'Here she comes!'
And that is dying.

*Henry Van Dyke* (1852–1933)

# The Wheel

Time is a wheel: the day that we met
Is still there:
Everything changes but nothing is lost
All that we shared,
All that we ever loved, belongs to us still:
Time is a wheel
Whatever has ended is just about to begin
All that we feel,
All that we ever felt, will come back again
Time is a wheel
The sound of your laughter, the rain in your hair,
Your hand in mine,
Your knock at the door, your step on the stair –
All are still there
Because time is a wheel and death will come round
As birth will come round
As love will come round, as peace will come round,
As joy will come round,
As life will come round, because time is a wheel
Bringing back, even yet,
All that we ever shared, and the day that we met.

*Susan Stocker* (1962– )

## *Live Your Life*

Live your life that the fear of death
can never enter your heart.
Trouble no one about his religion.
Respect others in their views
and demand that they respect yours.
Love your life, perfect your life,
beautify all things in your life.
Seek to make your life long
and of service to your people.
Prepare a noble death song for the day
when you go over the great divide.
Always give a word or sign of salute when meeting
or passing a friend, or even a stranger, if in a lonely place.
Show respect to all people but grovel to none.
When you rise in the morning, give thanks for the light,
for your life, for your strength.
Give thanks for your food and for the joy of living.
If you see no reason to give thanks,
the fault lies in yourself.
Touch not the poisonous firewater that makes wise ones turn to
    fools
and robs the spirit of its vision.
When your time comes to die, be not like those
whose hearts are filled with fear of death,
so that when their time comes they weep and pray
for a little more time to live their lives over again
in a different way.
Sing your death song, and die like a hero going home.

*Chief Tecumseh of the Shawnee Nation* (1768–1813)

## Prayer

Lord, make us instruments of your peace.
Where there is hatred, let us sow love;
Where there is injury, pardon;
Where there is discord, union;
Where there is doubt, faith;
Where there is despair, hope;
Where there is darkness, light;
Where there is sadness, joy;
O divine master, grant that we may not so much seek
To be consoled as to console,
To be understood as to understand,
To be loved as to love.
For it is in giving that we receive;
It is in pardoning that we are pardoned;
And it is in dying that we are born to eternal life.
Amen.

*St Francis of Assisi* (1181–1226)

## Old Irish Toast

May you have food and raiment,
A soft pillow for your head,
May you be forty years in heaven
Before the devil knows you're dead.

## For My Own Tomb-stone

To me 'twas giv'n to die to Thee 'tis giv'n
To live: Alas! One Moment sets us ev'n.
Mark! How impartial is the Will of Heav'n?

*Matthew Prior* (1664–1721)

# Notes

*p. 7* 'Death is nothing at all'. Henry Scott Holland was Canon of St Paul's Cathedral and a radical social reformer who campaigned for workers' rights.

*p. 31* 'Prayer'. Thomas Merton was a Trappist monk, based for twenty-seven years at Our Lady of Gethsemani in Trappist, Kentucky, USA.

*p. 33* 'The Serenity Prayer' is commonly attributed to Reinhold Niebuhr, although there is a question concerning its true origin. An earlier version seems to exist, published by Friedrich Christoph Oetinger (1702–82), a German theologian. However, it is Niebuhr's version that was popularized by Alcoholics Anonymous; it is placed at the core of their Twelve Steps and is printed on cards for members to carry with them.

*p. 35 Kindertotenlieder.* This extract is from the first of five poems set to music by Gustav Mahler.

*p. 66* 'Another and another and another'. James Henry was a Dublin doctor whose poems lay in the Cambridge University Library until discovered by the literary critic Christopher Ricks in the 1990s. Henry was fiercely opposed to traditional organized religion.

*p. 67* 'Fear no more the heat o' the sun'. *thunder-stone*: thunder-bolt. It was thought that the noise of thunder was made by meteorites falling to the earth.

*p. 75* 'The rooms and days we wandered through'. The last line translates as 'Do not be afraid, I am with you.'

*p. 77* 'You can shed tears that she is gone' was read at the funeral of Her Majesty Queen Elizabeth the Queen Mother, 9 April 2002.

*p. 94* 'don't tell me that I mourn too much'. Michael Rosen's poem is part of a sequence he wrote following the sudden death from meningitis of his eighteen-year-old son Eddie.

*p. 95* 'All Things Pass'. Lao-Tzu was a Chinese philosopher and reputed founder of the Taoist religion. He is credited with writing the *Tao Te Ching*: *tao* means the way of all life; *te*, the fit use of life by men; and *ching*, text or classic.

*p. 99* 'Gone from My Sight'. Henry Van Dyke was an American Presbyterian minister, literary critic and writer. In 1896 he published the hugely popular *The Story of the Other Wise Man*, which is about the fourth Magus and his journey to visit the newly born Christ child.

*p. 101* 'Live Your Life'. Tecumseh was a Native American chief who, with his brother Tenskwatawa, a religious visionary known as 'The Prophet', tried to unite the various tribes into an alliance against the expansion of the United States into the Midwest in the early nineteenth century.

*p. 102* 'Prayer'. The hymn 'Make Me a Channel of Your Peace is a version of this prayer by St Francis of Assissi.

# Acknowledgements

SIMON ARMITAGE: 'I thought I'd write my own obituary' and 'I've Made Out a Will' from *Book of Matches* by Simon Armitage. Reprinted by permission of Faber and Faber.

W. H. AUDEN: 'Funeral Blues' from *Collected Poems* by W. H. Auden. Reprinted by permission of Faber and Faber.

GEORGE BARKER: 'In Memorium E. S.' from *Collected Poems* by George Barker. Reprinted by permission of Faber and Faber.

OSCAR BEYNON: 'The New Path' by Oscar Beynon. By kind permission of the Jonathan Clowes Agency.

SIMON BRIDGES: 'Tomorrows' by Simon Bridges. By kind permission of the Jonathan Clowes Agency.

SARAH-JANE BROOKS: 'The Legacy' by Sarah-Jane Brooks. By kind permission of the Jonathan Clowes Agency.

NOËL COWARD: 'I'm here for a short visit only' and 'When I Have Fears' from *Collected Verse* by Noël Coward (Methuen Publishing Ltd, 1984). Copyright © the estate of Noël Coward.

ALAN CURTIS: 'Rest' by Alan Curtis. By kind permission of the Jonathan Clowes Agency.

WALTER DE LA MARE: 'Fare Well' by Walter de la Mare. By kind permission of the Literary Trustees of Walter de la Mare and the Society of Authors as their representatives.

HILDA DOOLITTLE: For UK and Commonwealth: 'Never More Will the Wind' by H. D. from *Collected Poems* by Hilda Doolittle (Carcanet Press, 1984). Reproduced by permission of Carcanet Press Ltd. For Canada: 'Never More Will the Wind' by H. D. (Hilda Doolittle) from *Collected Poems 1912–1944*. Copyright © 1982, by the estate of Hilda Doolittle. Reprinted by permission of New Directions Publishing Corp.

HELEN DUNMORE: 'I should like to be buried in a summer forest' by

Helen Dunmore from *Out of the Blue: Poems 1975–2001*, Bloodaxe Books, 2001.

DOUGLAS DUNN: 'The Kaleidoscope' from *Elegies* by Douglas Dunn. Reprinted by permission of Faber and Faber.

T. S. ELIOT: 'Home is where one starts from' from *East Coker, Four Quartets*, by T. S. Eliot. Reprinted by permission of Faber and Faber.

D. J. ENRIGHT: 'On the Death of a Child' by D. J. Enright from *Selected Poems* by D. J. Enright (Oxford University Press, 1990). Reproduced by permission of Carcanet Press Ltd.

VICKI FEAVER: 'Coats' from *Close Relatives* by Vicki Feaver (Secker, 1981). Reprinted by kind permission of the author.

ROBERT FRANCIS: 'While I Slept' by Robert Francis from *Collected Poems* (University of Massachusetts Press). Copyright by Robert Francis, 1976. Reproduced by permission of University of Massachusetts Press.

JOYCE GRENFELL: 'Life Goes On' from *Hats Off* (John Murray). Copyright © the Joyce Grenfell Memorial Trust, 1980. By kind permission of Sheil Land Associates.

DAVID HARSENT: 'Elegy' by David Harsent. By kind permission of the Jonathan Clowes Agency.

ASA JAMES: 'Think of Me Then' by Asa James. By kind permission of the Jonathan Clowes Agency.

ALICE KAVOUNAS: 'The Friend' by Alice Kavounas. By kind permission of the author.

LISA KITSON: 'Living Each Day' by Lisa Kitson. By kind permission of the Jonathan Clowes Agency.

PAUL MEADOWS: 'The Book' by Paul Meadows. By kind permission of the Jonathan Clowes Agency.

THOMAS MERTON: 'Prayer' from *Thoughts in Solitude* by Thomas Merton. Reprinted by permission of Curtis Brown, New York.

A. A. MILNE: Extract from *The House at Pooh Corner* by A. A. Milne. Copyright © under the Berne Convention. Published by Egmont Books Ltd, London, and used with permission. Copyright 1928 by E. P. Dutton, renewed © 1956 by A. A. Milne. Used by permission of Dutton Children's Books, a division of Penguin Young Readers

JO SHAPCOTT: 'When I Died' from *Her Book Poems 1988–1998* by Jo Shapcott. Reprinted by permission of Faber and Faber.

LOUIS SIMPSON: 'As birds are fitted to the boughs' by Louis Simpson. Copyright © 1998. Reprinted by permission of Louis Simpson.

SUSAN STOCKER: 'The Wheel' by Susan Stocker. By kind permission of the Jonathan Clowes Agency.

DYLAN THOMAS: 'Do not go gentle into that good night' by Dylan Thomas from *The Poems* published by J. M. Dent. By kind permission of David Higham Associates.

DEREK WALCOTT: 'Earth' from *Sea Grapes*, published by Jonathan Cape. Used by permission of the Random House Group Ltd.

JEANNE WILLIS: 'Inside Our Dreams' from *Toffee Pockets*, published by the Bodley Head. Used by permission of the Random House Group Ltd.

MARY YARNELL: 'Too Soon' by Mary Yarnall. By kind permission of the Jonathan Clowes Agency.